Hiding from Myself

Author
Martha Lazo-Munoz

Table of Contents

1. Beautiful Hope from Ugly Beginnings
2. The Friendly Neighbors
3. The Behaviors after Abuse
4. My Teen-age Years
5. A Young Bride
6. Divorced life back to School
7. Single Life
8. Longing for God
9. Living for God Marriage take two
10. Amazing Women came into my life
11. New Chapter in my life
12. Resources and Data
13. Sexual abuse prevention discussions
14. Trauma in Domestic Violence
15. Case Study's – Data
16. Where to get help
17. Job Training Programs

Dedications and Acknowledgments

To my beautiful family, that I adore! To my mother Leticia, who endured much heartaches to give her children the best as she knew how. The love and dedication as a single mother to her children and grandchildren, immediate siblings, sisters and to her community. To my beautiful children and grandchildren, you are most important to me, you are my "Why" I work so hard to be a better person, to be mindful of my life so that I may give back to the goodness of God. I wish to demonstrate that it is never ever too late to change the direction of your life! Thank you for your love, support throughout all my passions! Because of God's love for me that has made me a secure, whole and complete woman of God that I am today!

To my teachers, mentors, coaches and esteemed friends, pastors, clergy, Thanks for teaching me the value of study, research, prayers and meditations, and the importance of health and fitness, and to never give up on myself.

Additionally, it is God's love I want to share with the entire universe. My "why" I do and have done is for you to see that "all things are possible"!

I want everyone that reads this book to know and understand that there is a healing power available to all that believe.

Your life is not over until your last breath, and while we are still on this planet there is so much more out there in this world to see, do and become.

You can succeed! We, you and I were created for greatness! We each have a purpose for being alive.

My prayers are that you too find your calling and run with it. You just may save a life!

Last be not the least; to my husband who has been my rock for the last twenty years.

Through the highs and lows of our marriage and choosing to remain true to God and therefore true to me and our marriage. Actions speaks louder than words.

Furthermore, to my bonus family, I pray for you as well, may you also receive the love, joy of knowing that my desire for you is to experience the true meaning of healing, forgiveness and Gods love.

My husband and I both have learned the importance of serving our God, our lord Jesus Christ together, and demonstrating to our children that a life without God is no life at all within our homes.

Thank you honey, my funny valentine! Love you to the moon! #wriggly

Introduction

My "Why" I wrote the book and why I chose the cover. As an abused child, and a Domestic Violence survivor, I became someone else, as I was no longer a child. My innocence was lost and gone forever.

You want to hide, you mascaraed and become another person to not allow anyone to know your pain. You feel somehow, it's your fault, and it's not.

(Fact: PTS Takes place to protect yourself you focus on someone or something else) Your persona
(according to the NSPCC.ORG) It is stated: Sexually abused children can become fearful, "being frightened of some people, places or situations". I can identify with this characteristic.

My book cover was selected because I identified as a woman or child hiding most of my life, I hid behind doors, windows (so-to-speak) so that no one could see my real pain. My desire is to help those that have experienced or may have suffered any form of abuse, be it Domestic Violence, Child sexual abuse, Rape, Mental and or emotional abuse.

These issues and problems can scar you for a lifetime if one does not seek out help and the proper resources.

Seeking help from either a professional licensed psychiatrist, a pastor, clergy that are trained with these types of cases, and first and foremost it was God's love that worked for me with the combination of help.

Not everyone will understand and may attempt to give you what they think is right. This is an important part of the healing process.

I feel blessed my healing process took place as these amazing people came into in life at the right time. I choose to believe these amazing people were sent my way.

Disclaimer

This is my story, and I want the world to know this is not about blame. My Parents did the best as they knew how. I thank God for both my parents as they were selected to be my mother and father. This book is about how I found healing and was able to move past my pain and not have the "blame" game as many do. My hope and prayer are that everyone that reads this book will come away with a message of Hope, Encouragement, Faith and a sense that there is one greater that can and will help you. It does not matter what background, education status, nor where you come from, as this can happen to the most elite.

It's never ever too late to change the direction, the course of your life, and there is always an opportunity to heal.

My story is a life as it once was, and one I could not speak about until I was healed by Gods love, grace and mercy.

I emphasize again, this book is not about blaming my parents, nor family members. This is my reality as to what happened to me and how I healed and overcame my issues.

Chapter One
Beautiful Hope from Ugly Beginnings

The year was 1956 in El Paso, Texas a little baby girl was born. I was the second baby born to our parents. My parents were both hard working, so my older sister and I stayed with our aunt. She, our loving Tia (auntie) took care of us as best as she could since at that time, she had no children of her own, and was single and hadn't married yet. After four years my parents decided to move to Los Angeles, California, Lincoln Heights to be exact. Some of mother's family had moved previously to Los Angeles, Ca., as did father's family.

Mother at this point remained at home with us two girls, and shortly thereafter a third baby girl was born. I had several aunties, uncles and lots of cousins. I was still getting acquainted with them. We would often have family gatherings, bar-b-ques and sing along in our front porch.

Our uncles loved to sing and play the guitar. These songs have been in our families for years I suspect. The music was a Tex-Mex, (Texan) with a combination of Spanish folk songs, along with jazz in the mix. These were Amazing fun great experiences for sure! Music was part of dad's upbringing with his parents and siblings, as it became ours growing up.

A few years later, Dad had taken a trip to Blythe, Arizona to pick up our mother's family members. On their trip back home, our mom's sisters, cousins two girls, one of my mother's brothers, were hit by a drunk driver. Fortunately, most had gotten off the car and gone into a grocery store, but dad and my two cousins remained in the car. Dad got the worst of it! He was in critical condition, with several bones broken, and fractured ribs, one of his legs broken in multiple places, he was in a bad way for sure! I recall mother crying and so upset. She became so nerved and rattled by this horrific accident that by all appearances mother was in no condition to care for her children. I recall her sister; my aunt had to come and sit with us and take care of us. It was a strange time for us indeed, as I recall lots of people coming in and out of our house. I'm not to clear as to who were all these people and where they came from.

I just remember mother appearing in a foggy state of mind. I suspect mom was having a nervous breakdown due to all the stress. By the looks of things, it sounded like our father was not going to make it out alive. He was in grave condition. I don't recall the time frame as I was too young. With mother crying so much it was quite frightful for us as children. I remember being afraid as all the adults in the house were attending to mother's needs. Looking back now as an adult I get it; I fully understand some of mom's behaviors.

Our Mother became depressed, and such a sadness came upon her. One of the family members called a doctor and back then it as customary for house call visits. It appeared the doctor may have prescribed medications of sorts; I suspect anti-depressants perhaps?!

Although mother was a strong woman with such a determination, but I believe this was more than she could bare. Mother slowly would regain her strength and go on. Growing up and watching mom, she always demonstrated such strength. I believe she was a no-nonsense kind of gal or so she appeared. In some cases that is.

In other words, when things would happen (whatever that was for her) she would cry, be sad and then rise even stronger. I've been told by peers, colleagues and a few past bosses, "you just seem to pick yourself up even while facing difficulties" appearing almost like a nonchalant attitude. (learned behaviors I suppose) this is what has made me strong as well. At this point many months after dad's car accident, he learned how to play the trumpet, an instrument he so loved for many years! Since pretty much he was bed or chair ridden, it was difficult for him to walk with his severe broken leg, and since dad couldn't work his regular job and had fallen into some hard times with his ability to function with his daily routine job as a long shore-men welder. Father had been so proud of his welding job on ships, as I would overhear his conversations with my uncles, his brothers. He really enjoyed his job and was very proud. He had taken classes at a welding trade school and earned his certifications. He was a hardworking man indeed and most determined to provide for his family is what I remember most.

Eventually Mom had gained her strength, and was back to enjoying her cooking for the family and even a few of our neighbors would also join in. I recall mother acting more like her usual self. She appeared happy once again.

In my early years as a child I remember father was absent in our lives, he was on and off again. So, this became the norm for us at home. Although mother seemed to cry a lot and I didn't understand why. I'm not too sure if he was still in the hospital or if he just took another path. Our father would go in and out of our life's, so this was normal to see dad and the following month he was gone without word, or so it appeared that way to a child. Quite mysterious! As a child I recall feeling confused scared and very uncertain as to what was going on, or what was going to happen next. I didn't feel very secure growing up. It seemed as if there was always confusion of sorts.

I don't remember anyone of my family members attempting to comfort me, nor hug me and tell me it's going to all be alright. This is so important for parents to take note. Being sensitive and nurturing to your children. Especially when there's been an urgent matter, an accident, a death or some family ordeal. Children are confused, frightened and need to be comforted preferable by their parents, or a genuine family member, auntie or uncle. Being mindful of their fragile little hearts and minds. Show love, Gods love!

Chapter Two
The Friendly Neighbors

We had some neighbors, quite friendly, and while they had no children of their own, they seemed to love children a lot or it appeared that way. The man's name was Larry and his wife I don't recall. These neighbors seemed to hang around with us on occasions. Giving our mom groceries, and lots of goodies for us kids. A few years had passed mother had two more babies, again since father would come and go into our lives shortly thereafter fathers' visits mother would become pregnant. Mother was ever so busy with the new babies she did not have time to focus on older two, which was myself and my sister.

As children we learned to entertain ourselves. We enjoyed playing with our toys, bicycles and Jax. This game, Jax was with several silver little stars like, and made from metal, about eight to ten of them and a small little bouncing ball. You would toss the little ball up in the air and quickly attempt to pick up as many stars as you could. It was great fun for us girls and one of our favorite games.

I became quite good at entertaining myself. I loved to climb trees, jumping over neighbors' fence, running, skipping and playing jump rope. I was quite the hyper kid!

Reflecting, this is where I believe "doors" were open for the enemy to come in. (so-to-speak)

***Side Note*: The importance as parents to keep a close eye on your children. And to be aware with whomever your children stay with and or their whereabouts.

All this time I was being "groomed" by our neighbor Larry. Today I understand this term, "grooming" preparing a child just before sexual abuse happens.

Parents are also 'groomed' as they too are believing of these types of people, the predators. Abusers will often volunteer to babysit, pick your children up from school, and or watch the kids for a few hours while you're at work, or at the grocery store, or even just at home, or even at churches. As the neighbor Larry would take me into his garage, I just knew it did not feel right and he, Larry swore me to secrecy!

Often giving me candy or toys to silence me. This is typical of abusive men or women. They first begin to "groom" the child into thinking they are your friend. Predators will make you promise not to tell anyone as they will hurt you and or your family. Thus the "Fear tactic" takes place. This is where fear comes in, as children become fearful of what may happen to their loved ones. Abusers often are in the habit of giving gifts, telling your parents they care for you, buying you toys, and more. I thought this was the first of my abusive experiences but later I would learn it was also the very people I trusted! There was more abuse in my life as I remember. Our neighbor would not be my only abuser. I had blacked out or blocked out the other abusers since they were family.

Blocking out situations in your lifetime as they are often difficult to deal with. It's called a "safe mechanism" to self-protect oneself.

Children rely on their parents for their safety, as they are supposed to be your care takers, to protect you and shield you from any harm. The sexual abuse continued for many years on and off. Later I would learn it was various neighbors since we moved quite a bit. I recall feeling trapped, sad, lonely, confused, and most suffocated literally. By this time in my life I'm around the ages of five – seven, I think. I felt I had no voice, I wanted to scream but I couldn't, besides I felt who cared or who would help me. I recall feeling so scared most of the time. I was fearful of playing outdoors.

I had no one to rescue me, no one asked me how are you doing? All the while I was withdrawn, quiet at times, and at other times quite the hyper, and appeared as a defiant child that seemed unruly.

Side Notes: Parents take notes on your children. Be aware of their surroundings, who is playing with your babies? Watch and be mindful of your children's reactions while interacting with other adults, family or not. It is the responsibility of the parents to take good care of the children God has entrusted them to.

Chapter Three
The behaviors after the abuse

As I began to grow up, I had developed anger issues, depression and crazy dysfunctional behaviors. How could no one see this? I thought to myself. How could no one know what was happening to me? The dysfunction was evident as I look back. Why couldn't someone help me? Where were the adults in my life? Often abused children are withdrawn, and or have anger issues and or some form of acting out. These are some common signs to look for. Such behaviors or possible signs are lack of cleanliness, combing your hair, or brushing your teeth, and a sex appeal in young girls.

Side Notes: If your child is acting out with sexiness perhaps look deeper. With later years a sense of promiscuity can take place. (my personal experience)

Abused children are simply acting out, and or bullying becomes an issue, they can lack concentration and or isolation.

<u>Facts at: Helpguide.org</u>

What is child abuse and neglect: Child abuse is just not physical abuse it is also the neglect of a child or children. Ignoring children's needs, putting them in an unsupervised, dangerous situations, exposing them to sexual situations, or making them feel worthless or stupid are also forms of child abuse and neglect-and can leave a deep, lasting scars on kids. There are many forms of abuse, and signs to look for if you suspect a child or children are being abused.

<u>Side Notes:</u> These are all possible signs to look for. Pay attention to your children. Additional signs are;

if they are afraid to be with certain adults, and or family members, or daycare, pre-school. Notice if they are, fearful of going to school or certain places. If a parent stepfather or stepmother always insisting to babysit while you go to the grocery stores, church events. Other possible signs; are the children, teen's overeating? Or under eating? Food's often are used to cope with the pain. How's the child's health? Does he or she have health issues?

It is so important to pay attention to your child's behaviors and not just brush it off as "oh that's just how they are" please don't do that! In my early ages, I didn't want to be bathed, I didn't care much for combing my hair nor brushing my teeth.

Signs of depression had set in. I also did very poorly in school. I had a hard time focusing, learning, understanding. My thinking and thoughts were all over the place. I had learning disabilities, I was dyslexic, and slow in school. I was bullied, laughed at, made fun of because my shoes were dirty or old. These were my elementary school years. I was so fearful of people, and of life! I did not want to go to school as I was scared to tell anyone. One time I recalled either the school nurse, or a teacher drove me home, she spoke to my mother and told her I had head lice, and that I needed a bath. The sexual abuse was evident if only someone would have asked me why I was so withdrawn, and at other times so angry. I always felt as if I was the only child this was happening to. As the years progressed the molestations, and emotional abuse continued.

I think it was my 12th birthday when I recall saying "No more"!!! Something arose up in me and I do remember this much of saying "it is over"! no more shall anyone ever hurt me again!! I learned to hide, run from my abusers. I learned that if I was going to be abused, I could prolong it, as I ran to hide, sad but true. I now had developed a warped mentality, and I learned survival mode. I was now having to survive any attacks from my abusers. So, I learned to turn off my brain and think about beautiful things. I wanted to be a bird or butterfly so I could fly away.

(Yes, just like the movie) I had quite the imagination! I wanted out of my life! I was no longer going to allow someone to ever hurt me again and get away with it!! Since my abusers gave me something in return to not say a word, I learned to ask and get more. (survival mode)

In the evenings I would cry myself to sleep, and or I would cry in the shower hoping to be heard and hopefully mother would ask, "what is wrong"? but she never did. I often felt dirty, ugly and so unloved. I would ask myself "who cares"? no one I thought, so I learned to just suck it up! And suck it up I did for next ten to twenty years of my adult life! I had developed a coldness about me. I no longer had desires of anyone saving me, I had to save myself. (age twelve)

And suck it up I did over and over as the abuse lingered. The hidden anger was evident in my years that followed. I became the bully, and most active in sports, running, jumping, climbing trees. I believe this was a form of release for me. I felt free in running, swimming. These were the best things I could have done for myself.

A few times the neighborhood boys were bullying some of the girls as they walked home from school. I heard from inside the house and ran out after them with a baseball bat! No one was ever going to hurt girls again! Thus, I gained the respect from the neighborhood boys. I was the one being asked to join in on their baseball team. I did not dare share with anyone about my abuse for fear I would get in trouble or laughed at.

Often children that are abused think it's somehow their fault. The feeling of shame covers over you.

I often climbed trees and ponder how could I escape my pain permanently. This was my haven! No one could see me. My escape from the world as I could hide from everyone. I would look up and shed a tear or two and imagine I could fly away.

(Artwork by Katie Lazo @ klazoartist.com)

Chapter Four

"My Teen age years"

By age fourteen, I was tall, had long legs, and had curves in the right places, I had beautiful wavy long hair past my waistline. I knew I was pretty, or at least thought so because boys were now interested in me and whistling at me as I walked to school and back home. Although I was fearful, I rather liked the attention. One day after school, I insisted to my mother if I could go to my friend's house, knowing very well her older brother was having a party. I had no idea what a house party would look like, so of course I was quite interested. It was a chance to escape my daily routine of helping mother clean house and taking care of the younger siblings. My friend's older sister came and picked me up, and so it happened that while my friend gave me the tour of her home, I saw a young man just staring at me. I thought to myself, who is that old man? He seemed old for a house party, I thought it would only be high school kids. Well come to find out he was a senior at high school and that year he was graduating. I had no interest since he seemed much older than all the other boys. Making a long story short, he would later become my first husband. So, for about nearly one year I would become his girlfriend and he was my boyfriend. I was currently a young lady that had not experienced relations with a man. (other than molestation, which is still abuse, however no penetration). And thus, this friendship, relationship began to grow as time progressed., and at the age of sixteen (16) I became pregnant. My first experience and I would become a mother. (common for abused young girls to become pregnant as one becomes promiscuous due to the sexual abuse) Once I had announced I was pregnant we were both now saying to each other "what do we do now"? We were both so scared and wondered what we are going to do. He was a recent grad and making plans for his first year of college while holding down a job. I know he was just as scared as I was. He also did not have much family support either or so it appeared. He had a stern hard-working father and a mother that seemed absent emotionally. I didn't blame him as we were two young kids who hadn't a clue!

Chapter Five
A young bride

Before you knew it, we got married. The big wedding day came, and we had a traditional wedding celebration. We married in a catholic ceremony. The reception was huge, lots food, drinks and dancing. My family simply adored him since they felt he was quite the hard worker, a giver which indeed he was and is. At most family events he brought the drinks; beer, soda pop and whatever was needed. He was quite the gentleman, quite the charmer. Marriage at this age and because you are pregnant is not the solution to the issue at hand as it will only complicate life even more. But in our case, this is what we did, thinking it was the right. He was 22 years old, and I was barley 16 years old, we were both just two young kids that hadn't a clue about life, much less marriage. While it was evident, he dearly loved me, as he knew how to from his perspective, he would demonstrate this by buying me things, clothes, fancy shoes, any expensive makeup and things that are important to a woman. But marriage was not the answer nor the best way to go. How abusive relationships happen, it starts slowly and it's not always physical until the end. And so, it started within our marriage. I've come to understand and learned that abuse is a "learned behavior", and unless one acknowledges it and gets the proper help it will continue.

__Side note__: Variations of Abuse: There is the "mental and emotional games", as this plays with your emotions. This form happens by your partner not talking with you, ignoring you as you are not important to them and by not giving nor wanting to explain his or her whereabouts, the secret trips or vacations without you, not caring or showing his emotions for you, no or little actions of loving, caring or nurturing you. (or the private phone calls and hiding in bathroom or outside) "Physical" is just that; physical! It could be pushing, shoving, hitting, slapping and or actual punching you. (in some cases, even shooting you and or killing you) The worst of these it is stated the Emotional as it remains with you for years until you have completely dealt with it. Healing from such pain is a must, prior to entering another relationship. The emotional abuse came as the absence of my spouse, by not giving an account as to where he was nor where he had been, or with whom he had been and thus this became a norm. I did not dare ask him where he was for fear of what his reaction would be. (Do you see the resemblance from what my mother experienced with my father) Most of time he seemed happy, and I think it was with the numbing of the drinking. He could hide his true feelings; I suspect he was dealing with a lot of issues and could just not bring himself to talk about it to anyone. My understanding is that unhappy people or hurting people will hurt others.

We were destined to file for divorce a few years later. I see it now. My spouse at that time demonstrated excellent work ethics, he indeed was a hard worker, on some weekends he worked with his grandfather's construction business. He provided a beautiful custom built home, we enjoyed fun travels, fishing excursions on private boats since he was in a private fishing club, we would travel to many parts of Mexico, Cancun, Manzanillo, Loretto and Hawaii, we definitely enjoyed all the fun and wonderful family vacations, and amazing weekend rides to the local beaches, drives to the PCH or aka Pacific Coast Highway rides, but there was something within himself that he could not or would not share with me. As I look back, my ex-spouse behaviors and attitude reminded me of how similar my father's behaviors towards my mother. He worked a lot to provide for his family it just seemed as though he had a lot of overtime, and quite frequent. A hard worker indeed! When he was gone and no explanations,

(do you see the resemblance of my parents) I did not and would not ask questions about these behaviors after all I had everything and most material things any girl would want, and I was afraid to ask. Like my mother her abusive relationship with my father would be similar. Mother experienced the unfaithfulness, the adulterous affairs, the absences and lastly the physical and that did not go on as mother chose to separate finally and at last. And according to the world it seemed he, my husband was a great provider, a great guy indeed he was, and still is to this date. So why rock the boat right? Why complain? The hardest for me was the nights he would come home and wasn't feeling to well?! Or didn't come home at all. Drinking became an issue, I will admit I too was drinking with him on weekends, but when you continue drinking all week long that's an issue. So next what followed was the way I was handling my stress. I became anorexic, and drinking alcohol was not so appealing as I knew it would put on weight. I would not eat nor drink alcohol because this after all is a controlling issue. This was the only thing I could control. A form of self-punishment.

Repeatedly I would hear my family members say, "this is married life", deal with it, and after all look at what you have? This appeared normal and yet not so normal as I began to feel uncomfortable, sad and most depressed. I felt as if my family was more interested in what he was providing verses my feelings. So, I just went along with the program for a few more years. I began to want more for me, a normal family life without arguments and fighting. Somewhere deep within me there was an unsettling feeling, I believe that was God for one was tugging at my heart, and that somehow, I knew our life was in disarray. In my madness I began to work out a lot, I began swimming, lifting weights, and exercising like a mad woman. I just didn't want to feel pain anymore!

I also joined a gym, and a jazzercise club, this became my new addiction! My newfound passion, and for me my savior at that time. I was swimming a lot, and first thing most mornings while my children were young, I could very easily do 150-200 laps and not feel a thing! I think our pool was either 42' or 52' long, so this gives you an idea of the length of our pool or as I recall.

I was very thin for my height, 5'7" weighed about 127lbs. I didn't realize how thin I was becoming until one of siblings said, "oh my God you are so skinny". I however did not see it! I felt fat and out of sorts within my body. So, in addition to my daily routing, I felt the need to visit a church which was something we only did on special holidays, Christmas, Easter or Thanksgiving. I wanted more than just attending church on holidays, my soul was crying out for help.

All a while it was only a temporary band-aide. (so-to-speak) I tried reaching out to a clergy and he came out to visit us at home, he blessed our home and spoke to us about Gods love, and suggested we attend a marriage retreat with his church. And so, we did. It didn't work because neither one of us was willing to do the work, or we just didn't know how to apply what we had learned. We hadn't dealt with our pain or inner demons, nor our issues so how can or could have continued with our marriage.

Soon after it became more evident of my unhappiness and depression as well as his I'm sure. Weather he was having an affair or just not wanting to be home I just did not know. But I began to feel more and more alone, somewhat like a single mother. Interesting at how my mother also lived similar lifestyle. The dysfunction becomes part of the next generation until you deal with your issues. (What appears to feel or look like normal we accept it all a while it's not normal). Therefore, seeking help is so important. I believe everyone senses disorder deep within and either you do something about it, or you choose to live in denial, which I see many, many families do.

This was and is the very essence of Dysfunctional living! Moving forward my life took turns and twists, I now know this was part of the plan to grow and lean towards my Faith, and God.

"Our Mess is a Message" I've often heard this from the pulpit. We can share and teach others that are struggling with the same or similar issues.

- Understand God does not nor will he ever want bad or horrible things to happen just for his glory. On the contrary he will use what's happened to you to grow you and help others once you've healed. I suffered loneliness and sadness, I became anorexic and was deeply depressed! While the physical abuse came years later and not for very long as I chose another path for myself however, I did experience it. (hitting, pushing and shoving another human is not okay) this was the last straw!

Towards the end of our marriage, I felt near death within my issues. I knew I needed change, I needed help. I was not eating, and drinking alcohol later became my friend to fill my void, my loneliness. more abuse mentally and emotionally, and basically, I just wanted my life to be different but how? I hadn't had the tools nor the resources and most of my circle were all in dysfunctional abusive marriages as well. Most of our friends currently were going through similar situations. I had one of my dear friends, Linda and Mitch, my friend would confide that her husband would abuse her if she asked where he was. He was a 'functioning alcoholic', (and what this means, it's an actual term; is that one can be a drinker or a drug addict and still function and keep a job) So back to my friend, Linda., she too had the custom home as I did, and more money than she could spend. Shopping became our thing! We would have so much fun with our children shopping, going to the mall and bowling alley, and swimming at our home.

In the evenings or the weekends, we all would gather and bar-b-que while the kids swam. Linda would call me or come over quite a bit since both our husbands were gone at work. I suppose we were each other's support system without knowing it. I have often wondered if she remembers me, and how she is doing? Did their marriages survive?

A dear esteemed friend and my therapist Jonelle would say "Ages and Stages" at every age we go through various stages and that is so very true! This was the lifestyle we both knew and thought everyone lives like this, right?

Side Notes*facts: What is a Functioning Alcoholic and or Drug addicts: (The functioning drinker or drug addict can manage to appear normal and sober and, in some cases, even achieves success) They maintain their jobs or careers and provide for their families.
(visit alcohol.org)

<u>Domestic Violence is not okay! If you are in an abusive relationship, there is help. National hotline number: 1-800-799-7233 available 24/7</u>

Chapter Six

Divorced life back to school

Years later, I was about twenty – nine years of age or so and getting divorced with two teenaged kids and not a clue as to what was next. And since all those years my husband was my sole provider, I had minimal job skills and much less a career to speak of, incomplete education with no collage degree at that time, all I had was just the basic. I was so full of fear and very much dysfunctional and in denial. I was making poor choices for my life and is it was evident I was co-dependent. While I did not see it nor understand what was happening to me.

I thought perhaps going back to school might help me gain a great job to at least support myself.

Meanwhile a few years later I had decided to back to school and find a job. I would go on and later take classes at a local college. Additionally, attended seminars, and lectures in Sales, Customer Service, Zig Ziglar conferences, John Maxwell and a few others. Throughout my life I would continue to visit the Zig Ziglar meetings as I found Zig to be most resourceful and helpful as he talked about God and how he incorporated his God messages into his very own life. This I felt this was so empowering, here was this famous man and talking about God, I thought there must be something special about these messages as I was uplifted from my sadness and depression, even for that moment.

I learned this was a passion for me and enjoyed these conferences. Somehow at this stage of my life learning became enjoyable and easy. Years later I would attend the University of Phoenix. I earned Certifications from the University of Villanova, Six

Sigma-Quality Customer Service and studied the "curve system" which I found so fascinating. In all my madness and dysfunction, I loved to learn. But there was always still something so great missing in my life, me! How I was dealing with my inner self was not so good and I was determined to find out why. I was so out of sorts, and always feeling as if something was missing and just could not put a finger on it. I was lonely and depressed. I hadn't dealt with my inner demons not quite yet! (Some of the things I've learned throughout my hardships in life, if you are feeling out of sorts check in with God and please get help) (That's God talking to you).

I felt so empty, so invisible to the world and to myself. I was in horrible constant pain within myself, my soul seemed to hurt. (if that makes any sense)

Later learning that it's only God who can fill that void! The world hungers for love!

Although the world would see a different me, as I always seemed together and happy, I wasn't. I had a nonchalant attitude as if I could care less about anything or anyone, including myself. I was full of self, prideful and could appear to be cold. But deep within I was dying to be accepted by my family, friends and peers. My life as a single woman was not so cool after all.

I did miss having my husband around. I missed his strength, his amazing "let's travel adventures" I missed the good times. He was the solid rock, of our little family and I needed him! (But in reality, I needed God) He was controlling but at least I never had to worry about bills, mortgage payments, organizing our vacations.

And yes, he even cooked weekend breakfasts! (Stop what you're thinking, why did she leave him…abuse is abuse no woman deserves to be hurt and experience the: (honeymoon stages) this is the phase after you've been abused. The "Honeymoon" stage is where they make up with you, buying you gifts, traveling, loving on you etc. And while it does feel terrific until the abuse happens again.

Getting married at age sixteen didn't allow for me to be a teenager, to experience life. The pain was so great that I regressed to the age frame of mind when I got married. I didn't grow up as a normal teen-aged girl.

We were so young and hadn't learn how to deal with our inner demons, and unless two people are willing to get help and work together as a team it is impossible.

(healthy boundaries of course)

So, when I thought about going back, I would quickly recall the negative, and how it just didn't seem to fit anymore! By this time, I was in so much pain inwardly, the emotional, the mental pain of my depression were more than I could bare.

This is so typical of negative dysfunctional human beings (some judge people when you haven't a clue as to what's really going on) Please world, let's stop this insanity!

Some people may be suffering from mental illness, bi-polar, manic disorders, depressions, or recent traumas and yet society is so quick to assume everyone is on drugs. (not cool at all) Family to family, friends, neighbors etc. Dysfunction mindsets behavior's portray these behaviors.

The best suggestion I think, is to leave them alone, pray for people that are hurting and confused, while offering resources and tools and ask if you can help, never force the issue. (so, I've learned)

Move forward and stay on your own lane! Focus on you.

I saw plenty of people on drugs and I didn't care much for that, of course not knowing that alcohol is also a form of a drug as it numbs your pain, so is food, overspending, gambling and sex addiction. If it is governing, you or your body then that's a problem and you best get some help! Ask for help if you are ready to do the work. I always felt you can never ever let your guard down for fear someone will know your truth! (I said to myself) or take advantage of you. So, I went on with a facade of being strong, and independent to not allow anyone to ever hurt me again. But was I really that strong? Was I really self-protecting?

***Side Note* Unless one is healed, and you've done the work, and have had professional help you will always attract dysfunction into your life! I've seen it repeatedly with sorts of people. Various religious organizations are still in the same place as they have not done the work! Yes, God is there for you, however he gives you opportunities and resources. One must want to change it's that simple! (that's another book) These days I don't allow myself to get stuck or stay in one space if it is not healthy for me or my home life.

This includes family, stepfamilies, events, any social gatherings of sorts. I'm on auto pilot and if hearing malicious gossip or behaviors that rattle my core of who I am today, or my "being" I'm out of there! I feel my life has meaning and therefore I protect me, and my immediate loved ones. And you ought to do the same.! For the sake of your families it's important to Stop the insanity! This is so key to your growth in many ways. Be the example don't just talk about it.

Chapter Seven
Single life

My life had spiraled by this time. So, I became the life of the party! While my life seemed somewhat together the reality was, I was not, and I had begun to hurt myself by a lifestyle of disarray. I began to set out on a path that was so damaging to me. And while I thought I was hurting others which was my game, I was hurting myself over and over. This was my so-called revenge on the men that had abused me and robbed me of my innocence, now everyone would pay. All the while not knowing how to get off this sick merry-go-round! My life as I knew it was so dysfunctional, and I was a hot mess!!

My inner demons, my secrets were evident! And I was definitely "*Hiding from Myself*". I was truthfully so insecure and so mentally disorientated.

I felt I had no one, my family disowned me, and didn't want me at family events. (I don't blame them) but (Love covers a multitude of sin) where was the love? It is true, that if you don't love yourself why would others? I was sending out messages to the universe of how I hated myself, my life as it was. My journey at this point had been a rough one. A sad and tormented life. My journey would go on and my sickness, hidden secrets, sexual abuse and my failed marriage would take a toll on my life, and my children's life. The ones that suffer are your loved ones, your babies. But I didn't know any better. (not an excuse as this was what I knew) .

I always felt so proud that at least my kids were in a good place, as they had a stable home, and lacked no material thing, so in my viewpoint they were okay.

All awhile not knowing how much pain my children were in due to me and their fathers' poor choices and example-ship were affecting them too. They would suffer in silence. (children hurt by the parent's actions) I've learned to pray for people and come to understand that they too are suffering, in silence and we just don't know why. Be kind to people!

***Side Note** Depression, and Mental illness is evident, among abused children. This is PTS or AKA Post Trauma Stress. (Facts: "Here to help.bc.ca")

Childhood sexual abuse can have a wide range of effects into adulthood. Some adult survivors experience mental health problems, while others experience many health problems. Abuse is a kind of trauma. Trauma is a situation that's shocking, intense and distressing. The effects of trauma include a complicated factors, such as: The amount of any kind of trauma you previously experienced**The severity of the trauma**How close you were to the person who abused you**How long the abuse lasted**How people you trusted reacted to the abuse, if you told them, did they believe you and support you or dismiss you? One day while at a junior college, I met a woman. She was one of my teachers, and later would become one of my best friends, and my savior! As I enrolled for classes and uncertain as to what I wanted to take, my counselor suggested I take this class, and it was called

"Life learning skills" I had no idea what was in store for me. As it turned out my teacher was also a licensed family marriage therapist. As I began my class, I think she could see through me as I was distant, not fully paying attention at times, so she asked me if we could meet after class. Once you've learned about dysfunctional lifestyles it's obvious when you speak with someone or at least you get a sense something is just not right. You can almost zero in on certain behaviors just by asking a few key questions. As for me, not knowing what she had in mind, I agreed and thus my healing journey began.

**Side Note Once you become aware of Dysfunctional behaviors your more opt to be able to help someone else by offering resources.

She became one of my greatest friends, my confidante, and not only for me but for my entire immediate family. To this very day my adult children speak highly of her. God used her to help me, us. She was/is such a blessing in my life!! I will always, always be so grateful to her. She began to teach me words like: Dysfunctional, the Domino effect, Co-dependent and so much more! She became our therapist and worked with us for years. I felt like she was just a girlfriend I could turn to and just have a chat! One day she came to visit me unannounced and found me in such a way.

She lovingly and oh so gently reached out and took my hand and said I think it's time to go. I didn't understand where we were going., I assumed to her office. She had already been working with my health insurance company for coverage for a stay at a co-dependent center.

 She could see I needed serious help since I was harming myself with my out of control behaviors.

I will never ever be able to thank her enough for saving my life! This was only the beginning of my healing journey. I had so much more to go so much to learn throughout my life! I am so thankful for my teacher, my friend, my confidant! God works in mysterious ways! I phoned her recently, we chatted, and she so recalled my history. As we talked about the domino effect, the dysfunction within my family's histories. We agreed Unless one chooses these behaviors will continue onto the next generation. I adore her!

After completing my co-dependent program, I still had a lot to go through but at a minimum I had begun the work of healing somewhat. I learned key words that would help me understand and identify why I was so out of control.

I now had Resources; Tools I had never heard of! Thus, my healing began. But it would still be a long time for me to fully understand. A year or so thereafter, I began working at a non-profit organization where I helped people find jobs. I had prior experience working in this field, so it was not completely new to me. I became a Job developer and I loved it as it gave me a sense of worth, a sense of gratification and quite frankly I was good at it!

This type of job would go on the rest of my adult life. I worked with several organizations, groups and foundations and later became a Human Resources Regional Manager, where I was responsible for recruiting Nurse's and other healthcare professionals. I had earned my PHR (a certification for Human Resource Specialist) and continued to take classes.

I felt important and that my work was valued! I felt needed and wanted by my peers, co-workers and all those that I helped obtain employment. Later I learned how to work independently and under contracts with various non-profit organizations. And so, it was I would have my new-found passions and learned all about contracts. Financially I was feeling set! I could buy whatever I wanted, I loved shopping like Julia Roberts, in the movie "Pretty Woman" only I was buying with my own money that I worked for. I was doing quite well with my contracts, it seemed doors were just opening for me. I met so many wonderful people, and they were saying "yes" to me and my works. But there was still something missing, an emptiness, a void that was throbbing within me. While attempting to watch TV or have a quiet time, it was nearly impossible, as I had such a restlessness about me. I could not stand the quietness of my life at that time. So, what I did to help soothe my pain…spending money and lots of it. As quickly as I could earn it, I was spending it. My new-found passion was shopping! It was a great feeling to buy for myself but even better while shopping for my children and family. I felt validated somehow. As time progressed, I would visit my dear esteemed therapist from time to time. I still needed a lot of help emotionally, as I had not dealt with a lot of my hidden demons! I needed a savior! I needed God! Although my therapist was always available for me, but my needs were greater than any human being could ever offer. I needed a God intervention! While materially speaking I lacked not a thing, but deep down I was empty.

I always tried to keep busy so I would not feel my pain, but it was my pain I needed to deal with! My inner demons were still haunting me, and I didn't know what to do! I believe perhaps I reached out to my one of my sisters who would be my guide back to God. It's funny at how you just know exactly who to turn to for guidance of sorts. Do you know someone that just won't or can't sit still? Wonder what's really going on. Stillness is part of taking care of self, so I've learned.

Chapter Eight
Longing for God

I started to feel like I needed church, not knowing it was God, Jesus all along. I was re-introduced to Christianity by one of my siblings a while back, so I knew of God but had not developed a relationship with him. I had attended a Christian church but did not fully understand the trueness of God and how he really did love me. So, I went and visited a nearby church but didn't feel so excited or any breakthroughs like I had felt before. I was missing my sisters church, they always seemed to be an exciting fun bunch! A Pentecostal church go figure the excitement! This was for me! One day my sister called me out of the blue and asked me if I would go with her to church. I said sure, why not?

Well unbeknownst to me this church had been meeting at a night club I had once gone to, so I knew the location very well. I entered, and all these people were singing and clapping their hands, I thought what a strange church. And yet I had visited another location of this same church, but somehow, they were not as happy as this new location. Everyone started to pray in a funny and strange language, I thought what in the world? To not be different I closed my eyes, and something began to happen. Suddenly I was crying and could not stop the water works! I tried to stop crying but I couldn't. I could hear a woman howling with a deep cry, as it turned out that woman was me.

My sister so loving to put her arms around me and comforted me and said, "it's going to be alright" Gods got you now and you belong to him.

Thereafter my sister prayed for me and had me repeat some words and they were "lord forgive, I need you in my life, make me a new person, come into my heart" amen. Whew!!!!! What a feeling!!! I felt as if one thousand bricks came off me!! I felt free!! After that experience I knew this was for me. I knew I wanted this feeling always and never wanted to go back to my lonely life! I felt wanted, welcomed and somehow, I fit right in. All the lonely folk's hangout! (teehee) But it was more than that. A life without God is a lonely one. For me this is what I needed. I would begin my journey as a Christian and began going to church with my sister. It felt so good and so refreshing!

I loved going to church it gave me a sense of love and unity!

But not so fast! If you are not connected into a supportive bible study group or attending church regularly you are asking for trouble. (it won't work if you don't work it) It's like a muscle, you need to work it daily. I needed to stay connected and I found myself quickly making excuses.

My work was going so great, contract after contract I placed my job first. And soon after things just were not working out. God wanted my full attention and I wasn't ready for that. So off I went! My off and on relationship with God would be evident.

Side Note If you don't deal with your inner demons your past hurts and issues, anything can become addictive because you don't have complete healing or deliverance. Typically, it's denial of things that may have occurred in your lifetime.

I still had issues to deal with. I knew deep within my core I needed God twenty-four seven! Having hope and faith go hand in hand. This is and would be my balance forever! Denial is prevalent when one is or has not dealt with their issues. Some can attempt to hide it but if you look deep within at what they do or are doing; such as alcohol, drugs, sexual activities with multiple partners, overspending most of times it's a symptom of what is going on in the inside. I've learned over the course of my life as to what is good or not good for me. That is the importance of who's in your circle, who are you associating with? Are they positive folk's vs non positive, are they helping you to be better for yourself? I'm careful of who I allow in my circle. I'm so thankful for God coming into my life and helping me to get it right! He set my feet upon the rock! As I look back on my life it could only have been one way for me. Reflecting from the time mother took us to church and talked about God frequently it helped mold me. Throughout all my dysfunction and disarray in my life I did know the way out!

Chapter Nine
Living for God and Marriage take Two

Fast forward; God in his love and mercy knows and knew what I needed. While life would go on, it was about Ten to twelve years later I met a man that would become my second husband. He was funny, silly and mostly made me laugh. I enjoyed his company as he also enjoyed me. During the dating time I had no interests in anything other than remaining true to myself. The fact that he was caring for his elder father and had his frequent visits with his kids from his previous marriages, I was certain that he too was only interested in sharing some fun times with me and that was it. Meanwhile my life was full, I had given birth to the cutest ever little boy five years prior, my child would be my lifeline to God!! Because of him I wanted more for us both! I was content and had returned to school yet again, as this was my new passion, along with working. But boy of boy was I wrong! While he, my new husband to be, never said, nor ever mentioned a permanent relationship I was shocked when he said otherwise! He had five children, three adults and two high school kids that he frequently visited, and so I thought that he was cool dad. He had two children from his first marriage, and three from his second marriage. I would be wife number three. (I know what you're thinking; are you sure you want this guy, and red flag, red flag right?) One day out of the blue he states; "how about you take a walk with me down the aisle", I thought "what"??? Was he being his usual silly self, or was this guy serious? He had been divorced ten years prior to popping this question.

He was ready to settle down again with yet another wife. I was nowhere near wanting the same thing, after all my first marriage hadn't worked so why would this marriage work?

I just did not have any interest at all in getting married again, and the very thought scared me! I had so many fears! And honestly currently I felt like my life was good it was okay for the most part, and certainly didn't need to add anything else to the equation. We both had come from dysfunctional backgrounds, as it was evident and we both had issues and baggage for sure! It was evident by our life choices, and broken marriages. And our bible says; "you shall know them by their fruits" and oh boy was it evident in both our lives! This much I knew, that there still needed some serious work to be done within myself and with him too!! After all, why did he have two broken marriages? I wondered. I could understand one failed marriage but two? Wow! I thought! The RED FLAGS were coming up quickly! And although I could tell he hadn't a clue as to what the healing process meant, or that what needs to take place before entering into a serious commitment, he was oblivious to any of these terms I had learned. And obviously I wasn't living my best truth either at that time. I was still in my dysfunction and denial about my life. Again, running away from God's calling on my life! A onetime marriage breakup I could handle but a two-time divorcee was a tad much for me at that time. I thought, what is this guy is doing? And why would he want to get married so soon? I certainly was in no rush. I pretty much at that point was enjoying my life. But again, I would enter a marriage.

I chose to not pay attention to all the Red Flags! While it was fun times at first, but soon had challenging times in my new married life, but this time I turned to God like never, yet again! And fast!

I didn't waste too much time before I began to cry out for help! I knew I had entered an unhealthy relationship. I thought I knew what true love was or is. I loved him because he made me laugh, he appeared like the coolest guy ever and I felt I could fix any issues with him. I thought if I loved him the way he wanted; he would be the perfect man. (you cannot fix anyone but yourself) It's always easy to want to be the "fixer". I still was thinking with my old behaviors. Boy oh boy! Not again I thought.

Why did this happen to me again? Was I not healed from my past issues? With all my resources and tools, education, knowledge on dysfunctional relationships I had gotten myself into another relationship that needed healing. Sweet Jesus help me!! The only answer for me would be God. I had to relearn how to meditate and pray specifics, how to focus on me and my needs and that I had to rebuild my relationship with God first. "Walk by faith and not by sight" I would rehearse this verse over and over!! I relearned how to quiet my spirit, my soul and that everything would work out as they are meant to.

Letting go and allowing God to do his thing! And of course, don't get me wrong, I voiced my feelings, I set my boundaries and had plenty of times where we had time out within our marriage. Throughout the course of our marriage we separated a few times but each time he would come home with a different tone and new demeanor about himself. I had to trust the process and let go and let God for my marriage. My husband would end up spending time with a Pastor friend of ours in Denver, Colorado that helped him with certain man issues that he never spoke about to anyone. You see my husband had also experienced sexual abuse as a child and never learned the tools on how to deal with those memories that were still haunting him as an adult.

My husband would share with me about uncles he had and how he was taken advantage of as a young boy. His relationship with his father was not a healthy one.

He shared his father never demonstrated love for him, never hugged nor kissed as a father ought to. My husband also had endured abuse of sorts. He had to live with his grandmother as she was loving, caring and nurturing. He too needed to surrender his pain to God. (not that's it's okay to behave in such a negative manner) The attention he needed was God's love for him not other women.

I make no allowances. And so, it would be that he now too had surrendered his life to God and would be able to deal with certain issues as those rose up from time to time which caused his anger and other issues he had as a small child.

He came back home from Denver and was a humbler, a more understanding and sensitive man.

There were certain situations that were taking place within our home that were not acceptable to me and should not have been acceptable to him. But now he was a transformed new man of God.

After years of marriage and dealing with his personal issues he has become supportive of my endeavors, he also learned to pray for me and would ask God to grant me the desires of my heart. He began to pray daily and would read his bible early in the morning. He enjoyed sharing with me what he had read, and this became our morning routines. We would sit out in our patio during cool early mornings have our coffee, and discuss our day, and in the winter sit indoors with our fireplace going and cuddle with our warm blankets, while enjoying a cup of hot chocolate and marshmallows, and pray together. These were and are the best times of our marriage. This is essential for all marriages, unity together as husband and wife. Always work on keeping that type of fire going! Do the little things that makes you both happy as a couple and learn to forgive quickly, holding onto to anger to like poison to your own soul.

Although from time to time issues try and reappear, and it seemed he still had wild cats (so-to-speak) within him that needed to come out! I knew and could spot it quickly. So, I would gently embrace him and ask him to do you want to talk about it, and most times he did. We respect each other's space and healthy boundaries today.

Along with my boundaries of what is and not acceptable in our home, now it is understood the importance of prayer and surrendering his will to God. He too has learned about what resources are and tools, and how to effectively use them. And now as he has grown older, he is a loving gentleman. (don't get me wrong we both have our moments but at least we now know and understand how to work through them) And as life goes on one will always have somethings that attempt to come back into your life, but it's up to you to deal with it*!*

<u>Side Note</u>** *Set healthy boundaries for yourself. Talk with your spouse, or friendships and gently let them know if they've crossed the line. It's always best to discuss an issue when it's appropriate.*

One of my favorite quotes from my teacher, 'ages and stages' of one's life. As you grow older and mature you somehow become calmer, and or hopefully more aware. Those things that once bothered you are no longer issues. Today we are dealing with health issues for my husband. This explains some behaviors. With high blood pressure, high cholesterol and a diabetic disease these indeed trigger many of mood swings. Therefore, taking care of one's health is so important.

At times it frightens me as he is fourteen years my senior, but faith is in my God!

We have a good support system from our church members.

Without love and respect the chances of any marriage surviving will most likely non-exist. We don't allow the 'D-WORD" (divorce) to enter our vocabulary like before. What you speak will come forth. Therefore, speak life into your marriage and into your loved ones! Our goal as parents, grandparents is to promote healthy mindsets. By changing the way think and speak will manifest into your lives. Teaching the positive skillsets so that are children will become strong and God loving human beings. Our adult children can see how we deal with issues and work quickly to resolve. Forgiveness is key in any relationship. Holding onto anger is not healthy. And besides what are you demonstrating to your circle, be it family, friends, neighbors or the world?

Side Note Statistics for second marriages, and third marriages, are a small amount of survival. A blended family is most challenging. Be prepared! Do your homework! The children and or grandchildren may not easily accept stepparent. The children although adults are still dealing with the effects of their parents first marriage. It is stated: the 60% of second marriages will end in Divorce. 73% of third marriages end in Divorce. The United States has the 6th highest divorce rate in the world. (data research)

Dysfunctional opposing parent can continue to be adding poison to the children or even adult children's minds, it is most difficult to have a healthy relationship. The opposing parent wants to control and manipulate the children, even if they are adults.

This is a form of abuse and control. (these are learned behaviors) (narcissistic behaviors) it's all about control issues. The opposing parent still has unresolved issues within herself, or himself. It's all about them and their wants and needs, and to somehow hurt the opposing parent. Some of the adult children think this is acceptable behavior and often say "that's just how mom or dad is" all a while they are still in a controlled and manipulated abusive relationship with one of the parents.

This is called "Dysfunction". These adult children are dysfunctional and as sick as the parent, because it's an ongoing unhealthy relationship. Dysfunctional families and some parents encourage adult children to side with them, and or are always finding faults with the opposite parent. Not realizing they are or were just as sick and dysfunctional as their previous partners. Stop the blame game and look at yourself. "get rid of your own log or plank from your own eye" (bible vs. Matthew 7:5) In other words look at yourself before placing judgement on others.

In my dealings with broken marriages, abused spouses I'm often told of some of the stories they go through, as the other parent wants full control although some are adult children of divorced families.

They choose not to see how unhealthy these behaviors are, and or not sure how to handle this. Thus, a learned dysfunctional behavior becomes the norm within the families. I choose to stay away from such families or gatherings as they attempt to spread toxin to everyone that will listen to them. Dysfunctional and Narcissistic parent is rude and insists on her way or his way. Listen to the conversations and you will quickly hear where they are coming from. A DYSFUNCTION and NARCISSISTIC mouth. (No thanks)

**Side Note A healthy relationship with both parents comes to play when all the family members are willing to do the work. Stop the insanity! If you are finding that one of the parents is still blaming the other parent, assess the situation and ask yourself; "is this healthy". "Is my parent still trying to control me"? am I adult enough to correct this parent and tell them the truth? Work on self-first is key! Be that example to your family and friends.

"The truth will set you free"!

Our prayers are, that we are the example to our children, grandchildren on how God can save a marriage. While by far we are not the perfect couple, and will always have various issues from time to time but at least we are not where we use to be. And we will always seek out help, we choose to change in order to have a healthy positive life. You can't force anyone, he or she must want change. We pray for love, peace and unity within our blended families and for the next generations to have healthy relationships.

Chapter Ten

"Amazing Women came into my life"
And
"Identifying your Purpose"

Years later in my life, I have met some *Amazing Women* that have/and had helped me along my journey. These women would help me by encouraging me to believe in myself. The continuance of one's education is vital for growth and development. We must not ever stop learning and be teachable. Surround yourself with positive people who demonstrate example-ship of sorts. Learn all about Mindsets, why we do what we do, it's learned behaviors. You want to surround yourself with women that will pray, uphold you when you can't uphold yourself. Surround yourself with women that have had similar experiences and how they have worked through their issues of sorts and are now successful in whatever that means to you. Never stop learning and growing! Look all around you there are winners and champions everywhere! Don't get stuck always be evolving. As for me I enjoy traveling and seeing new places and meeting new friends. The type of work I chose allows me this, and this amazing lifestyle. I can basically work from anywhere around the world! Perhaps this is you?!

Identifying your Purpose

Within all these years I knew or always felt I could own my own business. I've always enjoyed helping others with job development and assisting with finding their careers. Perhaps you have a book within you? How I found my own calling was by helping others. I recall sharing with previous mangers my thoughts or ideas only to be told "this is how we have always done things" or "not interested in your ideas" but I always said, "why not"? Well years later I would find out "why not"? God was setting me up for my own business. Sometimes doors closed are an opportunity for you to find what you are good at. There was always a sense of wanting to own my business. I have always been in the "helps" ministry if you will.

From the time I was a little girl, I enjoyed helping people. If some of my friends were hungry, I'd bring them home since mom always had a warm pot of hot stew cooking, beans, tortillas and or sweet bread aka pan dulce (Spanish) for sweet bread. I enjoyed sharing! Back tracking here a minute, I recall at one of my jobs I had met a woman that co-partnered with us, approached me and asked me if I would be interested in contracting with her agency. I had never heard of this before. She was the first to introduce me to "Contracting". I was re-introduced to this idea. Second time around! (Gods trying to tell me something) this would help me find my purpose. Things began to make sense. Suddenly I was back at it again! Interesting! I began to yet again revisit how to start my business. As I asked other women that were handling contracts, I found this was perfect for me.

All a while I know that God had been preparing me. This woman I met was teaching me the pros and the cons and said she would work with me and help me; she would become my sub-contractor. I gained yet another mentor, my guide for new resources I needed. This woman apparently had worked with one of my Directors (possible she too was sub-contracting) All I knew was I loved it! My job, my contract was to find employers that would hire our applicants and the benefits to the employer would be to receive Tax credits and half the salaries paid. What a concept!

As you begin to align yourself with God, and your purpose he will guide you and show what your calling is. We each have a purpose in life. There is always something special within you to do for this universe! So yet again this would happen to me over the course of my life. Follow your heart, follow your dreams. Never place the keys of your happiness in the hands of others! I am Pro healthy body, mind and soul! I encourage you to have mentors, coaches and teachers of sorts. My goals and aspirations are to share with others how to take ownership. "No one can hurt you unless you give them permission". (Eleanor Roosevelt)

Today I enjoy researching and sharing with other women, girls of all ages how to work through their issues. And basically, isn't that what life is about? Helping each other?! Back then I just couldn't have imaged helping anyone else while going through my pain.

My life was one great big pain and mess! I thank God for giving me the strength to get through and where I am today!

Chapter Eleven

New Chapter in my life

New Chapter in my life! 2019 is the best yet ever!! Today I am new woman! I know that for me it was and is my God, Jesus Christ. I believe in his love; I believe he is the creator of this universe. He gives me such a peace in my soul. I've learned to pray and meditate in the mornings. I declare and decree the good things for my life and my loved ones! I believe you have the power to call out those things you desire (in a healthy way of course) "For God so loved the world he gave his only begotten son, that whosoever believes in him, he will be saved". John 3:16.

I choose to believe he, Jesus healed me, changed my stinking thinking, he set my feet on the right pathway. I am eternally thankful and grateful for my life today! Looking back on my life I think 'what a mess' and yet this is what happened to me to get where I'm at today.

I want to be that voice for the women of all ages, and to the children, letting them know that someone does care. I want to share and talk about eating disorders as well, and how some turn to food for their pain, comfort. How food is also a tool that one

may use to hurt themselves. Review this within your own lives. I know as it once was me too.
To the parents that just don't get it……abuse or any issues with their children, giving tools and resources. I now know what my job is and that is to share my story, and give hope, faith and love.

As that saying goes, "you can lead a horse to water, but you can't make him drink" and that is so true!! I also now believe that I was born for such a time as this. All things work together at the right timing! Today my husband and I are working on leaving a legacy to our children and grandchildren, with a message of love, hope and possibilities. We desire for them to not ever give up their hopes and dreams. And mostly deal with inner issues so that you're not in unhealthy relationships of sorts.
As for me, my life is not my own. I strongly desire to be of service to God and help with Domestic

Violence and Sexual abuse issues. Bringing awareness, the laws that need change.

There is so much work to do in this universe we need to be a positive solution. Sex trafficking is at it's all time high! We need to be a voice of whatever that means to you.

I am excited for life! I possess a zest and a zeal!! I want women all over the world to know that God loves them, and he has a plan and a purpose for their lives. (Jeremiah 29:11 "for I know the plans that I have for you, plans to prosper you and not to harm you", by following his words. Believe it!!

If you were an Abused child, it's not your fault! You did nothing wrong to deserve that! Work through your pain and your hurts with a licensed, a knowledgeable clergy or pastor that can give you sound advice. Your pain is real! Your fears are real! Learn how to overcome these and you too can live a victorious life!

Chapter Twelve

Resources, Data and Facts

Facts on Abused Children

https://defendinnocence.org/5-facts-child-child-sexual-abuse/

BELIEVE THE CHILD: HOW TO BE SUPPORTIVE WHEN A CHILD BREAKS THE SILENCE

When a Child Discloses Abuse

At Defend Innocence, a program we hear a lot of stories from parents about their experiences. Some are funny, some are empowering, and some are heartbreaking. The ones that are among the most heartbreaking are when a child came to the trusted adult in their life and told them they were being sexually abused, and the adult didn't believe them.

Perhaps the person abusing them was an admired figure in the community, or a family member, or a close friend. Perhaps it was just easier to believe the child was lying than to confront the reality of THAT person doing THAT to a child.

According to <u>Darkness to Light</u>, it's estimated that only 4 to 8 percent of child sexual abuse reports are fabricated. And of those, most are made by adults involved in custody disputes, or by adolescents.

A child who has been sexually abused will be afraid, confused, and traumatized. It is unlikely that they are lying and more likely that they have used all the courage they have to break the silence and tell you.

Whatever the reason, when you disbelieve a child sharing something so horrible with you, then you empower the perpetrator to keep doing it. Any time you silence the child, you make it safer for sexual abusers.

Believe the Child Give them that benefit of the doubt and be a safe person for them to talk to and confide in.

CHAPTER THIRTEEN

SEXUAL ABUSE PREVENTION DISCUSSIONS TO HAVE WITH YOUR CO-PARENT

A single mom recently asked us how she could get on the same page as her children's father and their stepmother when it came to talk about healthy sexuality. She wanted to introduce topics in both households so that the children had continuity in what they were learning.

A dad recently joked that his wife handled all the talks and he wasn't sure what his children were learning about healthy sexuality, or if they were.

Another couple disagreed on what should be taught to children and when. They weren't sure how to decide who was right and who was wrong.

For all these situations (and a few others) creating an open dialogue with your co-parent will make all the difference in the world. It will allow you to make sure that your child is getting consistent messages across the board and nothing is getting left out of the little talks you're both having with him or her.

Here are seven things to talk to your co-parent about:

1. When will the talks take place?

We are big proponents of having frequent little talks instead of one big talk. That's important information to make sure you both understand. Make it clear that ANY time is a good time to have conversations about healthy sexuality, consent, sexual abuse, etc.

2. Topics you'll discuss.

It's important that you talk about what will be covered with your child at what age. If you're teaching your child the proper names for their body parts, will that start when they're potty training or earlier? When you talk to your child about dating, will that occur when they're 10 or closer to a teenager?

3. Phrases and wording.

Make sure that you're using the same words and phrases as your co-parent. If at mom's house they learn about "uncomfortable touch" but at dad's, it's labeled "unsafe touch," there might be some confusion.

4. Who will address which topic?

It's good for children to hear about healthy sexuality from all the important adults in their life. There may be some things that you think would be better coming from your spouse. Let them know that you'd like them to take the reins on that discussion.

5. Values you want to address.

Depending on your political, religious, or personal beliefs, there may be certain viewpoints that you want your child to be aware of during your discussions. Make sure that you and your partner respect each other's values and are comfortable with them being shared with your child.

6. Look at your circle of trust.

This is something that you should address together as well. Your child will trust who you trust. Are all the people with unfettered access to your child individuals that you want around him or her? Are there person(s) or people that you want your child to be wary around? Discuss this together before you ever bring up safety issues with your child.

7. What you don't know.

It's important to plan for what will happen if your child asks a question for which you don't know the answer. One way is to plan another conversation for after you've found the answer for them. Plan so that both parents handle this situation in similar ways.

No matter the parental situation in your child's life, there is a way for all parents to participate in the conversations about healthy sexuality. Get all the adults together and discuss these topics.

Chapter Fourteen

Trauma Domestic
Violencehttp://earlytraumagrief.anu.edu.au/files/mezey.pdf

Domestic violence, lifetime trauma and psychological health of childbearing women

Gillian Mezey, a Loraine Bacchus, b Susan Bewley, c Sarah Whites

Objective Although histories of abuse are associated with psychiatric illness in women, health professionals rarely enquire directly about such experiences. This study examined the association between physical and sexual violence and lifetime trauma and depressive and posttraumatic stress symptoms in women receiving maternity care.

Design Cross sectional study. Setting South London Hospital maternity services. Population Two hundred women receiving postnatal or antenatal care. Methods Two hundred women receiving postnatal or antenatal care at a South London maternity service were screened for lifetime experiences of trauma and domestic violence. Information was obtained about self-harming behavior, suicidal thoughts and attempts and psychiatric history. Women completed the Edinburgh Postnatal Depression Scale (EPDS) and the Posttraumatic Diagnostic Scale (PTDS). Main outcome measures Results One hundred and twenty-one (60.5%) women reported at least one traumatic event and two-thirds of these had experienced multiple traumatic events.

The most frequent (34%) was witnessing or experiencing physical assault by a family member. Forty-seven (23.5%) women had experienced domestic violence. Physical and sexual abuse commonly co-occurred. Thirteen (10.7%) women with a trauma history had current posttraumatic stress disorder. Severe posttraumatic symptoms were associated with physical and sexual abuse histories and repeat victimization. Adult and childhood physical and sexual abuse histories were also associated with more severe depressive symptomatology. Significant social factors associated with depression were being single, separated or in a non-cohabiting relationship. Conclusion Traumatic events are under-recognized risk factors in the development of depressive and posttraumatic stress symptoms in childbearing women.

Childhood abuse creates a vulnerability to traumatization in adulthood. Awareness of the impact of trauma and abuse on psychological health may enable more appropriate targeting of clinical services and support for women receiving maternity care.

INTRODUCTION TRAUMA

It is recognized that severe or life-threatening trauma is a risk factor for the development of psychiatric illness including posttraumatic stress disorder and depression.1 According to the Diagnostic and Statistical Manual for Mental Disorders (DSM-IV), a traumatic event is defined as one 'that involves actual or threatened death, serious injury or threat to physical integrity' and gives rise to feelings of intense fear, horror or helplessness.[2] The risk of developing posttraumatic stress disorder following a traumatic event depends on a number of factors, including the type of trauma, and is highest following assaultive violence.[3] Although women are at less risk than men of being exposed to major or life-threatening trauma, once exposed they are twice as likely to develop posttraumatic stress disorder.[4] Women also experience different kinds of traumatic events to men; with higher rates of sexual and domestic violence, which are associated with the highest rates of posttraumatic stress disorder.[5] Domestic violence is under-reported and under-recognized across a range of health settings.[6] Health professionals rarely enquire about domestic violence and women are reluctant to disclose such experiences in the absence of direct questioning.[7,8] A number of studies have found that, once exposed to a traumatic event, the risk of experiencing a subsequent trauma is substantially increased. Women who have been sexually abused as children are significantly more likely to report subsequent abuse as an adult, including domestic violence, than women without a childhood abuse history.10 It is possible that domestic violence acts as a marker. Department of Mental Health (Forensic), St George's Hospital Medical School, London, UK b. Women's Health Academic Unit, Florence Nightingale School of Nursing and Midwifery, King's College London, St Thomas' Hospital, London, UK c. Women's Services Directorate, St Thomas' Hospital, London, UK

Correspondence: Dr G. Maze, Department of Mental Health (Forensic), St George's Hospital Medical School, Jenner Wing, Ground Floor, Cranmer Terrace, London, UK. Other traumatic and adverse life events, which mediate the psychiatric and social difficulties that are often attributed to domestic violence. However, what is not clear, is whether the risk of re-victimization relates exclusively to physical and sexual violence or whether it is increased for all types of trauma, outside the context of interpersonal violence. Studies of depression during pregnancy and the postpartum period have generally failed to assess for histories of abuse and violence as potential risk factors,[11,12] in spite of the suggestion that women may be particularly vulnerable to domestic violence during this time.[13] This study was part of a larger ESRC funded research project on domestic violence in pregnancy, which was carried out in the maternity services of two South London teaching hospitals.

The aim of this study was to examine the prevalence and types of traumatic events, reported by women and the impact of the various types of traumatic events on women's mental health, particularly with respect to posttraumatic stress disorder and depression. The study received ethical approval from St Thomas' Hospital Research Ethics Committee.

METHODS

The study used a cross sectional design that consisted of 200 English-speaking women, aged 16 and older, from the postnatal and antenatal wards and the Day Assessment Unit (antenatal) at Guy's and St Thomas' maternity service between July 2001 and April 2002. As the primary aim of this study was to estimate the prevalence of domestic violence in an obstetric population, the study was powered to be able to estimate the prevalence within an acceptable error margin. Therefore, it was planned to recruit 200 patients to be able to calculate the 95% confidence interval around the estimate of prevalence of domestic violence to within F5%. Researcher (LB) that the research was to assess women's health during pregnancy. Women who agreed to participate were taken to a private room away from the wards where they were given a full explanation of the study. Women were informed that all information was confidential, unless they indicated that there was a risk of harm to an existing child. Participants were offered a £10 gift voucher in recognition of their assistance. All women who participated in the research were offered contact cards with information about local organizations that offer support to women experiencing domestic violence. Additional time was given to women who disclosed domestic violence and wished to discuss this further. Women were also asked whether they wished any disclosure of domestic violence or abuse to be communicated to a health professional.

A semi-structured interview included questions about demographics and psychological health. Civil status was coded as a dichotomous variable: 'married or cohabiting' and 'single, separated, cohabiting relationship'. Ethnicity was collapsed into three categories due to the small numbers in some ethnic groups: 'Black', 'White' and 'other'. Employment was coded as 'in paid employment/on maternity leave' or 'unemployed/in receipt of sickness benefit'. Socioeconomic classification was derived using the Standard Occupational Classification, Volumes 1 and 2[14,15] using the categories: 'managerial and professional occupations', 'intermediate occupations' and 'routine and manual occupations (including the long term unemployed)'. Experiences of domestic violence were assessed using a variation of the

Abuse Assessment Screen.16 Women who reported physical or sexual violence by a current or former partner/husband or family member were coded as positive for a history of domestic violence. About psychological health, women were asked whether they had ever consulted their GP complaining of 'nerves, anxiety, sleeping problems, or feeling sad', if they had ever received a psychiatric diagnosis from a health professional, and treatment they were offered. Dichotomous 'yes/no' questions were used to elicit information about self-harming behavior, suicidal thoughts and suicide attempts. Women were additionally asked to complete two self-report psychological measures.

The Edinburgh Postnatal Depression Scale (EPDS) is a 10-item scale to assess depression, which was originally developed for post-natal use,17 but is now validated for use during pregnancy.18 All women were asked to rate on a four-point scale how they felt in the preceding week in response to the 10 items. A cutoff score of 14/15 was used antenatally, as recommended by Murray and Cox18 because of the high levels of dysphoria in pregnancy, and 12/13 postnatally.

Chapter Sixteen

Where to get help

Millions of Americans are victims of domestic violence.

Most abuse survivors tell someone about the violence, but fewer find the right person to help them. National and local organizations provide victim services online and in person.

Hotline.Org the National Domestic Violence

1-800-799-7223

They speak over 200 (two hundred) languages around the world.

Spotting Abuse

One challenge is that abuse may not always be obvious, as domestic violence researcher Christine Murray points out. "One of the defining characteristics of an abusive relationship is that one partner is trying to control and hold power over the other person, and they use the various forms of abuse to gain and maintain that control," says Murray, who is a member of the American Counseling Association and Associate professor in the Department of Counseling and Educational Development at the University of North Carolina at Greensboro.

The following behaviors by a partner can be signs of an abusive relationship:

- Keeping constant tabs on where you are, what you're doing, who you're with.

- Preventing you from seeing friends or family

- Threatening or intimidating you

- Destroying your possessions and or Threatening your pets

What to Do if You are in an Abusive Relationship

**Get to a safe place where you can call for help

**Is the abuser nearby? Does he/she have a weapon?

**Contact local law enforcement agency immediately

**Get to a shelter and or a friend's home while arrangements are **being made for a shelter

**File "stay away or restraining orders" Typically court houses have **support to assist with filling out and or completing documents, and **all necessary paperwork. You will need to make inquires, ask, set **up appointments. Second parties such a local law enforcement, or **any induvial over the age of eighteen, and or a certified mail will **work with the court systems to "serve documents" to defendants.

**If you have children check and be sure they are okay mentally, **emotionally and or physically.

**Get counseling from a licensed certified expert that can help guide **you. You've experienced trauma of sorts. Local churches can help **with spiritual guidance and offer comfort in times of need.

**Support groups are key for venting, sharing and supporting one **another.

There is hope! Keep the faith!

Visit us @ www.womenslegacyofhope.com

martha@womenslegacyofhope.com

Mailing address: 12227 Bear Valley Rd. #284
Apple Valley, Ca. 92308

Chapter Seventeen
Job Training Programs

Once you've completed your programs, Domestic Violence Healing, Court Systems, counseling etc. We offer the Job Training programs.

Often in Domestic Violence cases and or other situations one may stay in an abusive relationship due to lack of work experience, not having a college degree or lack of skills.

We work with most Job Training job sites and can assist with Referrals and Tools to obtain a job and or a career. "It is essential to be in a place of calm and peaceful environment for effectiveness while on the job training and or school settings". We offer this help in most states. (by appointments only currently)

"With God All things are possible"
(Jesus Christ- Matthew 19:23-30)

Martha Lazo-Munoz
I Am Women's Legacy of Hope
www.womenslegacyofhope.com

"Hiding from Myself"

Made in the
USA
Middletown, DE